The Circulatory System

Walter Oleksy

the rosen publishing group's
rosen
central

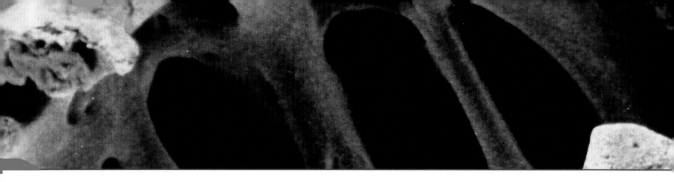

Published in 2001 by The Rosen Publishing Group, Inc.
29 East 21st Street, New York, NY 10010

First Edition

Library of Congress Cataloging-in-Publication Data

Oleksy, Walter G., 1930–
The circulatory system / by Walter Oleksy. — 1st ed.
       p. cm. — (The insider's guide to the body)
Includes bibliographical references and index.
ISBN 0-8239-3336-9 (library binding)
1.   Cardiovascular   system—Physiology—Juvenile   literature.
[1. Circulatory system.] I. Title. II. Series.
QP103 .O445 2000
612.1—dc21

                                                                00-009417

Manufactured in the United States of America

Contents

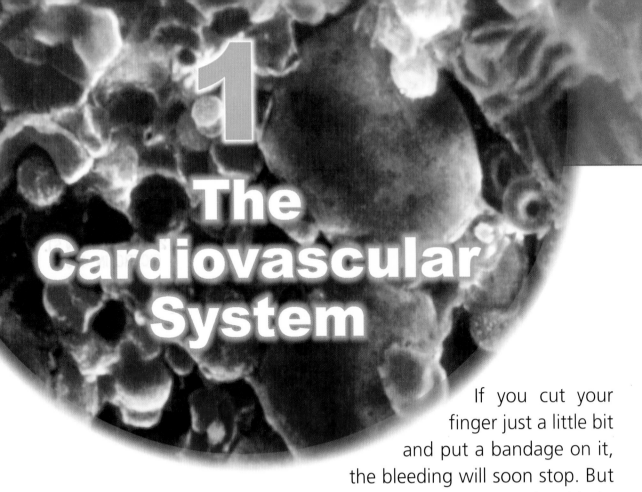

1
The Cardiovascular System

If you cut your finger just a little bit and put a bandage on it, the bleeding will soon stop. But even before the bandage is applied, substances in the blood help it to clot as soon as it is exposed to air. After the cut has been bandaged a while, the cut heals and the skin fuses together again. In the meantime, a scab forms to protect the cut until new skin can grow over it. But what is this stuff called blood, and what does it do for you?

Blood is a very important part of why and how you are alive and healthy. And the blood itself is part of and needs to flow through a circulatory system. The circulatory system, which is also known as the cardiovascular system, keeps your heart beating and your blood flowing around your body. It supplies the cells of the body with the food and oxygen they need to sustain life.

All animals, except for the most simple, primitive ones, have some type of circulatory system. The human circulatory system consists of the heart, which acts as a pump; the blood; and a branching network of tiny flexible tubes called blood vessels.

The heart acts as the pump of the circulatory system, allowing oxygen-rich blood to flow through the body's arteries and veins.

Blood Vessels

There are three main types of blood vessels: arteries, veins, and capillaries. Arteries carry oxygen-rich blood away from the heart to all parts of your body. Veins carry blood back to the heart. Capillaries are the tiny blood vessels that connect the arteries with the veins.

The blood in your circulatory system also carries your body's hormones. Hormones are produced by the endocrine glands such as the thyroid, pituitary, adrenal, and sex glands. These glands release their hormones into the bloodstream. These substances control the activities of various organs and tissues that help your body to function properly.

Blood also keeps your body healthy by defending it against infections. And it takes away the waste products in your body such as carbon dioxide and urea, which are flushed out of your system to keep you healthy.

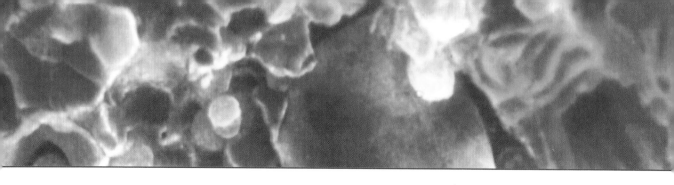

The circulatory system is made up of two components. Systemic circulation serves the body as a whole except for the lungs. Pulmonary circulation carries the blood to and from the lungs.

Early Knowledge of the Circulatory System

Doctors and scientists who lived and worked thousands of years ago were aware that the heart and blood are essential to sustaining life. Egyptian anatomists living about 3,600 years ago discovered that vessels went from the heart to all parts of the body. But they didn't know that blood passed through those vessels. Ancient Greek philosophers believed that a person's soul was carried through their blood.

Hippocrates (460–377 BC), who is called the father of medicine, believed that the body was made up of four substances called "humors." These were blood, yellow bile, phlegm (mucus), and black bile. Bile is a bitter liquid secreted by the liver that aids in digestion. The Greeks believed that if the humors were not functioning in balance, people became ill. Other Greek philosophers such as Plato (428–347 BC) and Aristotle (384–322 BC) believed that life came from a kind of spiritual fire. It was a "flame of life" that burned in the heart. Food nourished the flame, while breathing in air kept the fire under control.

An ancient Greek doctor, Galen (AD 129–199), believed that life was sustained by a mysterious substance in the air called the pneuma. After it was breathed in through the mouth, the pneuma supposedly passed through the blood vessels in the body to the heart. There it cleansed and vitalized the blood. At the same time, pneuma took away the body's waste substances. Galen's beliefs weren't right, but they were accepted as late as the 16th century, when Italian anatomists made substantial discoveries about how the heart pumped blood.

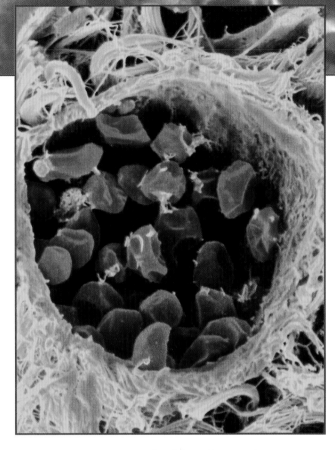

A cross section of a blood vessel in the lung. Red blood cells pick up oxygen in the lungs and transport it to tissues throughout the body.

Realdo Columbus (1516–1559) found that there is a separate system of blood vessels, besides those that supply the body, that supplies the lungs. Andrea Cesalpino (1519–1603), though he did not discover the way that the heart pumped blood, became the first to call the body's blood transport system "circulation."

A major breakthrough in understanding the circulatory system came in 1628, when the English doctor, William Harvey (1578–1657), discovered that blood was pumped by the heart and flows around the body in a circular motion through a system of vessels. While

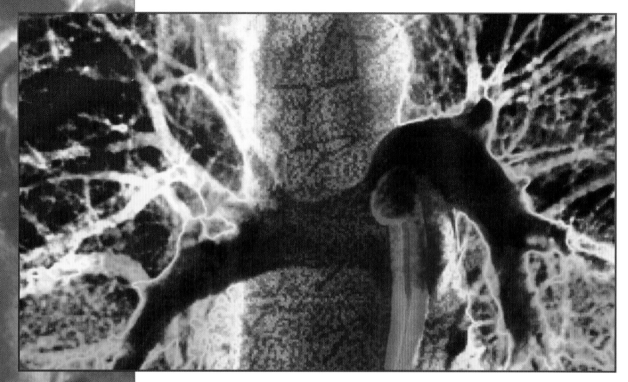

The pulmonary arteries transport deoxygenated blood from the heart to the left and right branches of the lungs.

Harvey learned that blood flows in one direction only, the Italian anatomist, Marcello Malpighi (1628–1694), later discovered the connecting capillaries between arteries and veins by making microscopic studies.

The Path of the Circulatory System

The cycle of the circulatory system begins when blood passes through the right side of the heart after passing through the lungs and being renewed with oxygen. This blood is pumped into the aorta, the largest blood vessel in the body. After the blood leaves the aorta, it travels through a system of smaller arteries and finally passes into the capillaries. These tiny vessels send blood through all the tissues of the body, supplying the body's cells with nutrients and oxygen. At the same time, the blood collects waste matter from the cells in the body, including carbon dioxide gas. When all its oxygen supply is used up, the blood moves into the veins and travels back to the heart.

When the oxygen-depleted blood reaches the heart, it is pumped through large vessels called pulmonary arteries and sent to the lungs. The blood then undergoes a cleaning process in the lungs. Carbon dioxide is exchanged for oxygen in a process known as oxygenation. The blood is now rich in oxygen again. It flows back to the heart through the pulmonary veins. Another cycle of the circulatory system begins instantly.

Help from Other Systems

The circulatory system does not just work by itself. It needs help from other organs in the body. The circulatory system works in close coordination with the respiratory system. The two systems interact when the blood pumped by the heart passes through the lungs.

Another essential partner of the circulatory system is the hematologic system. This system builds blood cells in the bone marrow, and includes the lymph nodes and the spleen. To more fully understand the circulatory system, let's learn more about blood and the heart, and how they work together to keep us alive and healthy.

2
The Heart

Basically, the heart is a hollow muscle that acts as a pump. The heart's function is to propel blood on its journey through the body. Tiny tubes called blood vessels carry blood from the heart to every tissue and organ of the body such as the brain, lungs, and kidneys. The heart itself has a system of blood vessels that bring it oxygen. The heart's blood vessels are called coronary arteries and veins.

The Heart's Left and Right Pumps

The heart has two separate pumps that lie side by side. The muscles of these pumps relax when they take in blood and contract as they push blood out. The left side of the heart is a stronger pump than the right side. The left pump receives blood from the lungs and sends it to cells throughout the body. The right pump receives blood from these cells and sends the blood

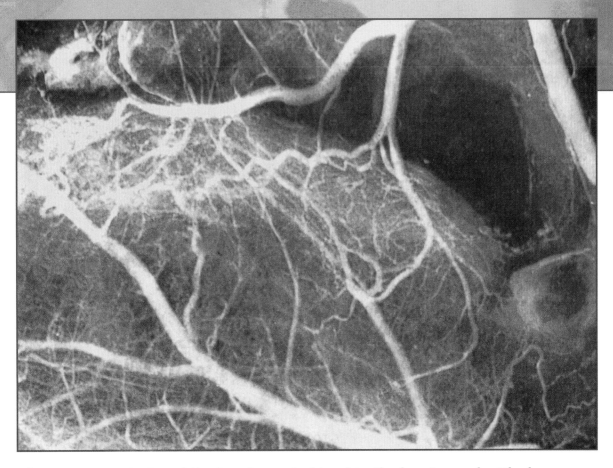

The coronary arteries of the heart supply blood to the heart muscle. Blockages in these arteries can lead to heart attack, stroke, and death.

back to the lungs. The right pump sends oxygen-depleted blood along the pulmonary artery to the lungs. There the blood gets rid of carbon dioxide and picks up a fresh supply of oxygen.

Blood then returns to the heart's left pump by way of the pulmonary vein. The left pump then sends the blood along the aorta and other arteries and out to the entire body. The blood delivers oxygen to the body's cells and gathers carbon dioxide. It then returns along the main veins to the heart's right pump. This cycle is repeated endlessly.

FACTS ABOUT THE HEART

- Your heart is just a little to the left of center in the middle of your chest.
- The heart is made up mostly of special muscle tissue called cardiac muscle.
- A heartbeat is one complete contraction and relaxation of the heart muscle. This usually takes less than one second.
- The heart beats or contracts about 70 times per minute or about 100,000 times a day. That amounts to 2.5 billion times, if a person lives to the age of 70.
- The heart of an adult human is about the size of a fist. In men, it weighs about 11 ounces (310 grams). In women it weighs about 7 ounces (200 grams).
- Your circulatory system contains about 5 quarts (4.7 liters) of blood. Your heart pumps about 7,200 quarts (7,500 liters) of blood around the body each day.
- The aorta is the largest artery in the body. It is about one inch in diameter.

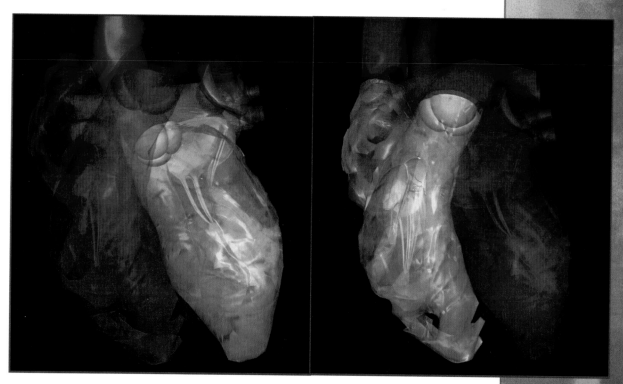

The chambers of the heart are highlighted above. The picture on the left features the left atrium, and the picture on the right features the right atrium.

Getting to Know the Heart

The heart is located between the body's two lungs. It is just to the left of the center of the chest cavity, which is called the thorax. The human heart has four chambers. The upper part of the heart holds the right atrium and the left atrium. These atria are two almost round chambers that receive blood. The atria help the heart to pump blood by contracting just a fraction of a second before the ventricles do. The ventricles are the two main cavities of the heart below the atria that receive blood and propel it into the arteries.

The heart has three layers of tissue. A thin inner layer lines the hollow chambers of the heart. The middle layer is thick and muscular. The outer layer is thin, with a fatty covering. A thin protective shield called the pericardium surrounds the heart. It is made up of two delicate layers of connecting tissue. These are separated by a very thin layer of lubricating fluid. The pericardium allows the heart to expand and contract billions of times without creating any friction or interfering with other nearby parts of the body.

The heart's muscle cells are not like the cells of other muscle tissues. Most of the muscle cells in the heart are grooved or striated. Striated muscle cells, like the cells of skeletal muscle tissue, are usually under the conscious control of the central nervous system, like the muscle cells that contract when you decide to take a walk. But striated heart muscle cells are not under voluntary control and move without direct stimulation from the central nervous system. In this sense they are more like the smooth or nonstriated muscle cells that control our digestive tract and other involuntary functions of the body. You don't have to think about it to make your heart beat.

Heart Valves

A heartbeat is the sound your heart makes when its valves open and close. The valves of the heart are strong but flexible membranes that keep the blood flowing through the blood vessels in one direction only. The valves are located between the upper and lower chambers of the heart and in the main veins. As blood is sent to the heart, the valves open to let the blood flow in the correct direction. But when a chamber of the heart is full and the heart contracts, the valves shut. This stops the blood from flowing the wrong way.

A heart valve can become loose, frayed, or otherwise damaged. Then it doesn't close all the way, and lets blood flow in the wrong direction. Doctors can replace a damaged valve with an artificial valve or one donated from another person. The heart valves of some animals, such as pigs, can also be used to replace human valves.

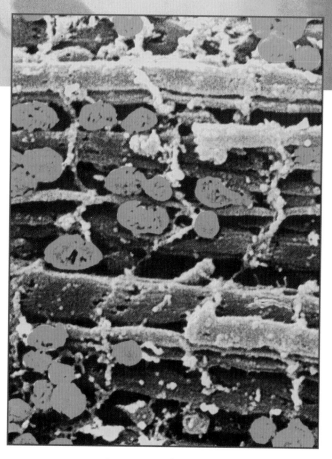

Heart muscle fibers, shown here in green, are supplied with energy by the mitochondria, shown in red. The heart muscles continuously pump blood throughout the entire body.

Modern Heart Miracles

In recent years, doctors have been able to replace a damaged or diseased human heart with either an artificial, mechanical heart, or a healthy human heart. In preparing for their death, many generous people donate their hearts for transplantation to others in need of them. In the future, transplant hearts may not only come from humans but from some animals. This may become possible through genetic engineering.

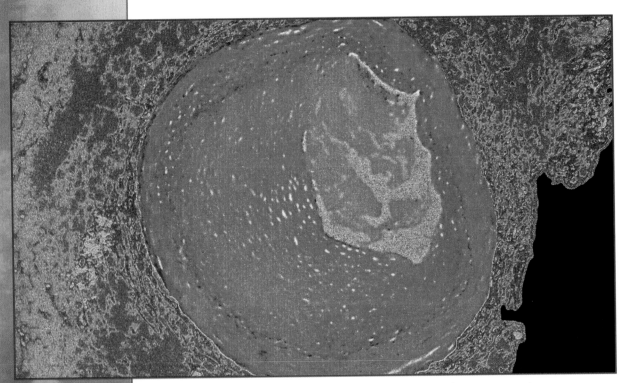

This blocked coronary artery, shown in red, is severely narrowed by plaque deposits. Blockage, which is typically caused by smoking or poor diet, can lead to heart attack or stroke.

Another modern miracle for people with damaged hearts is the pacemaker. It is a battery-operated device that helps a heart to beat with a steady, healthy rhythm. Heart specialists usually place a pacemaker under a patient's skin at the shoulder. It is connected to the heart by wires. The newest pacemakers each contain a microchip, such as those used in computers. The chip varies the heart's rate according to the patient's needs.

Coronary arteries can also become blocked by the buildup of deposits of cholesterol and fat. Doctors now can treat a blocked coronary artery by building new blood vessels as detours around the blockage. This is called heart bypass surgery.

In bypass surgery, a less important blood vessel, such as a vein from one of the patient's legs, is removed. Doctors then sew the vessel onto the coronary artery on either side of the blockage. By rerouting the blood so it can flow to the coronary artery, the heart's muscle gets the nutrients and oxygen it needs to function properly.

Try These Experiments

Every beat of your heart is sparked by tiny electrical signals sent to your heart's muscle tissue by nerve cells. Surges of blood caused by every heartbeat make the walls of the arteries bulge. These bulges are the pulse you feel when you place a finger on blood vessels that run near the surface of your skin.

Want to see how your heart beats? Here's how. Just press two fingers onto the inside, or palm side, of your wrist. Feel the pulses? That's your heart beating. You also can feel it beating in your neck, your ankle, the top of your foot, and your groin. To see how many times a minute your heart beats, you can count the number of times you feel a surge in your blood vessels. This is called taking your pulse.

The best way to do this experiment is to feel on the inside of your wrist, below the thumb. Place three fingers (not your thumb) in the hollow next to the tendons that run up the middle of the wrist. In a little while, you will feel the pulse beating against your fingertips. Count your pulse for one minute while you are sitting down. Then run in-place for a minute and take your pulse again. Notice that your pulse is faster after you are more active.

Now let's learn more about the blood in your circulatory system.

3 Blood

Blood is the life-sustaining fluid that circulates in the arteries, veins, and capillaries of humans and many other animals. It is essential to life and plays an important role in every major activity of the body. One of the main functions of blood is to transport oxygen from the lungs to the body's cells.

Blood contains millions of tiny cells, most of them red. Mixed in with the red blood cells are the less numerous white cells. The average adult's body contains about 70 milliliters (2.3 ounces) of blood for each kilogram (2.2 pounds) of body weight. This means that an adult weighing 70 kg (154 pounds) has about 5,000 milliliters, or nearly five and a half quarts, of blood.

Blood travels in a continuous cycle through the body. It is forced through the blood vessels by the pumping action of the heart. Besides supplying the body cells with oxygen and removing their wastes, blood has several other important functions. It distributes food, vitamins, and enzymes to the cells. It also carries hormones from the endocrine glands to the tissues and organs.

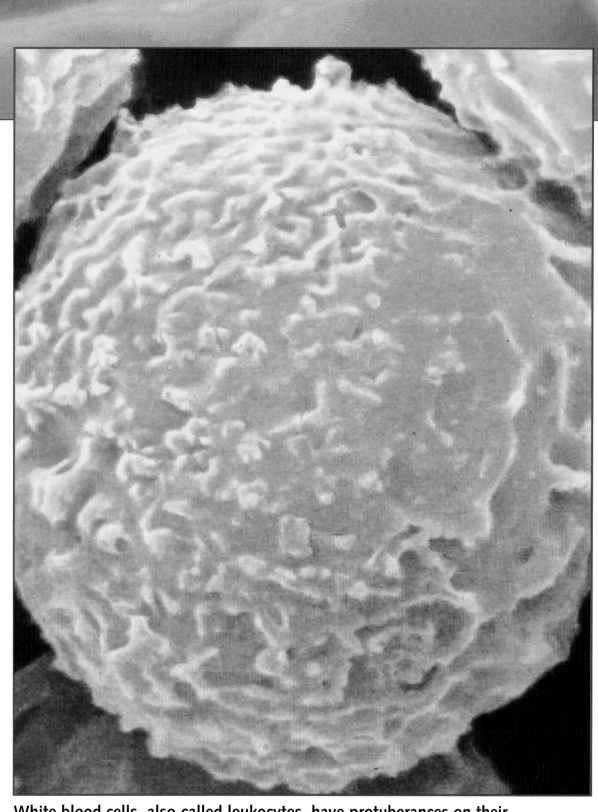

White blood cells, also called leukocytes, have protuberances on their surfaces that enable them to move to areas where they can engulf foreign invaders, such as bacteria and viruses.

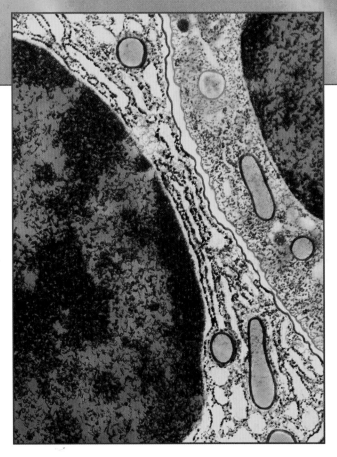

Plasma cells are mature white blood cells that secrete, or release, antibodies in an immune response.

Blood protects the body against infections. Some blood cells attack and destroy bacteria. Other blood cells produce antibodies, special proteins that react with bacteria and neutralize their harmful effects. Blood also helps to control the body's temperature so that it is neither too hot nor too cold. Blood does this by absorbing heat when it passes through the active organs of the body. It then releases the heat when it passes through tissues near the skin.

What Blood Is Made Of

Blood may look like a simple red liquid, but it is actually a body tissue. The cells, instead of being joined together as in solid body tissues, are suspended in a fluid. The fluid part of the blood is called plasma. Plasma is made up mostly of water, but it also contains proteins, minerals, and other substances. Plasma makes up about 55 percent of the blood. Blood plasma is made up of about 91 percent water, 8 percent organic compounds, and 1 percent inorganic substances.

The organic compounds are mainly proteins. In recent years, scientists have discovered that when blood is in short supply, plasma substitutes can be used to restore the blood volume in some emergencies. However, there is no perfect artificial substitute for plasma. The cellular part of the blood is mainly made up of red blood cells, as well as smaller numbers of white blood cells and platelets.

Red Blood Cells

Red blood cells carry oxygen and carbon dioxide throughout the body. They make up most of the cellular portion of the blood. There are about 5 million red blood cells in each cubic millimeter of blood in most adult men and 4.4 million per cubic millimeter in most adult women.

If you study red blood cells under a microscope, they look like tiny round or slightly oval-shaped discs. To some, they even look like tiny doughnuts. Each red blood cell contains molecules of a red-colored chemical called hemoglobin. Hemoglobin is a chemical that holds oxygen molecules after they leave the lungs. The outer membrane of a red blood cell is very elastic. This allows the cell to change its shape as it squeezes through tiny, narrow capillaries.

Try this experiment with capillaries. Press hard on a fingernail with the thumb of your other hand. See how the flesh under the nail turns white? That's because you're squeezing blood out of the capillaries in your finger. When you stop pressing on the finger, its normal pink color returns as the blood flows back.

Red blood cells live for only about 120 days. As they wear out and age, they are captured and disposed of by cells in the spleen and other organs. Most of the materials from the destroyed cells are recycled to form new cells.

White Blood Cells

The body contains a lot fewer white blood cells than red cells. But white blood cells are very important because they protect the body against infection. They do this in two ways. They engulf and digest bacteria, old cells, and other foreign bodies. They also produce antibodies to attack and destroy germs.

White blood cells are different from red blood cells in several important ways. Unlike red cells, white cells are complete cells. They are larger than red cells and have a nucleus. White blood cells are not just carried by the bloodstream. They also can move about independently. They also can move out of the bloodstream. They do this by squeezing between the cells that line the walls of the blood vessels.

Platelets

Platelets, or clotting cells, are the smallest blood cells. They measure only from one to two microns in diameter. Platelets are round or oval-shaped and are named for their plate like shape. Like red blood cells, they have no nucleus. There are about 300,000 to 400,000 platelets in each cubic millimeter of blood. Platelets are important in the process of blood clotting, which prevents the body from losing excess amounts of blood. When a blood vessel is cut, platelets adhere to the rough surfaces of the cut. They release substances that then help the blood to clot and stop the bleeding. The process of blood clotting is called hemostasis. After they form in the body's bone marrow, platelets circulate in the blood for about nine days and then die.

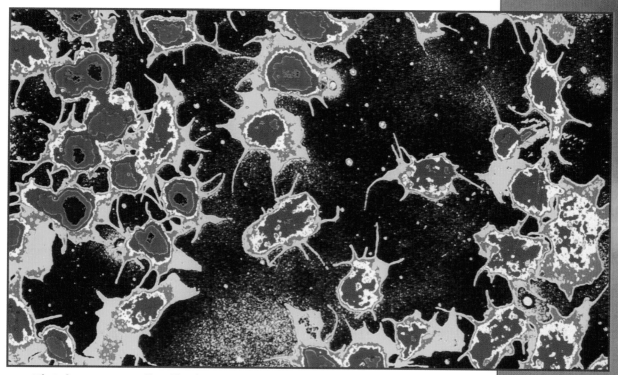

Platelets are small cells that circulate in the blood after forming in the bone marrow. Platelets help to plug defects in the walls of small blood vessels and help blood to clot.

What Blood Type Are You?

If you are injured and lose blood in amounts that require a blood transfusion, it is important for doctors to know what type of blood is in your body.

Before the twentieth century, doctors thought all human blood was the same. When they tried to replace lost blood, the patients often died because the wrong blood was put in their system. Around 1901, Karl Landsteiner, an Austrian-American doctor of pathology, the study of human diseases, discovered that there are four major groups of blood. This discovery led to the ABO system of blood classification and the beginning of a new and safe way of giving blood transfusions.

The ABO system is based on the fact that some people have what is called type A blood and some people have type B blood. Others have type AB or type O blood. If the wrong blood type is injected into a person, the blood will clot and cause death.

In 1940, Landsteiner and an American pathologist, Alexander S. Wiener, discovered another system of blood grouping that they called the Rh system. They named it after the rhesus monkeys they experimented on. People with Rh+ or Rh- factors in their blood have or lack a certain protein, and when transfusing blood, doctors have to match Rh factors as well as blood type.

Everyone should know what blood type they have. In an emergency involving severe bleeding, paramedics will need to know what type of blood you might need. If a person's blood type is not known before getting a blood transfusion, a simple blood test is made to determine what type blood they have.

Blood Transfusions and Blood Banks

It is often vitally important for the success of an operation or the survival of a patient for doctors to replace or restore blood in a person's system. A person gets new blood in their circulatory system by means of a blood transfusion. This is usually done in a hospital where blood in a container slowly drips through a tube and through a needle into a vein in a patient's arm.

Hospitals collect and store blood for these emergencies in what are called blood banks. These banks receive "deposits" from blood donors, healthy people who are willing to donate their blood to others. Hospitals select blood donors and determine their blood types. This guarantees that the new blood a patient receives matches the blood in their system. The blood people donate to hospitals

has to be carefully handled. Sometimes anti-clotting elements are added to make sure that the blood does not clot after it is taken out of the donor's body.

The practice of storing blood for transfusions began in hospitals during World War I in 1918. An American doctor, Oswald H. Robertson, found that blood could be safely kept for several days at temperatures just above freezing. However, it wasn't until 1940 that the first large-scale blood bank was established, at the Cook County Hospital in Chicago. Since then, blood banks have become available at hospitals worldwide.

Millions of healthy adults voluntarily give some of their blood to hospital blood banks each year. However, the need for blood is always great, especially when people are injured in catastrophes such as earthquakes, tornadoes, and fires. Human bodies seldom need all their blood, and since blood replenishes itself regularly, it is safe for people to donate some of their blood for others in need.

When the Body Loses Blood

Parts of the blood are continually being destroyed. However, the blood volume in our bodies stays constant. About 1 percent of our red blood cells die every day. They are replaced by new red blood cells. Portions of the plasma also disappear, but are constantly renewed.

If blood is lost—for example, through a hemorrhage—the body rapidly attempts to restore the lost volume of blood. This process starts with fluid passing automatically from the tissues into the blood vessels. After a while, the production of blood cells is increased. If the body loses large amounts of blood, a condition called shock occurs and may cause death. Serious burns can also cause shock.

Facts About Blood

Your body contains about 25 trillion red blood cells. A teaspoonful of blood contains about 25 billion red blood cells. There are between 20 and 55 million white blood cells in your body. Your body also has about 1.75 billion platelets. Capillaries are so thin that ten of them together would be a lot thinner than one of the hairs on your head.

Blood travels through the body very quickly. It leaves the heart at about three feet per second. It slows down as it enters the smaller arteries. It takes about a minute for a drop of blood to travel from your heart to your toes and back again.

At any point in time, 64 percent of your blood is flowing through your veins. Twenty percent more is pumping through the arteries and

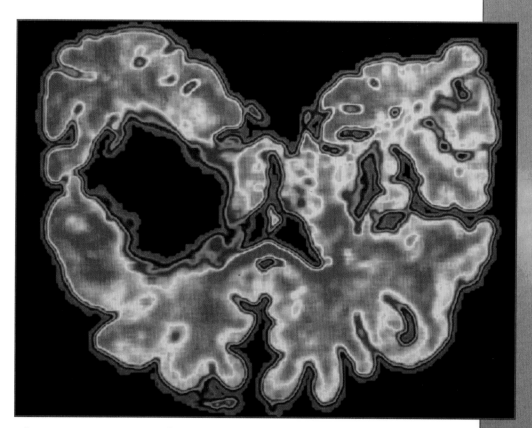

This is a computer-enhanced image of the brain. The black area on the left shows a large accumulation of blood, which was caused by a stroke.

capillaries around your body. Another 9 percent is in your lungs, and the remaining 7 percent is flowing through your brain. Blood is red because it contains a colored substance called hemoglobin in the red blood cells. The iron in hemoglobin gives blood its red color.

A child has about three quarts of blood in his or her body. An adult has about five quarts, and a baby about one quart. The kidneys get more blood than any other organ; they filter it and clean it. The length of all the blood vessels in your body—veins, arteries, and capillaries—is about 60,000 miles. That is nearly two and a half times the distance around the world.

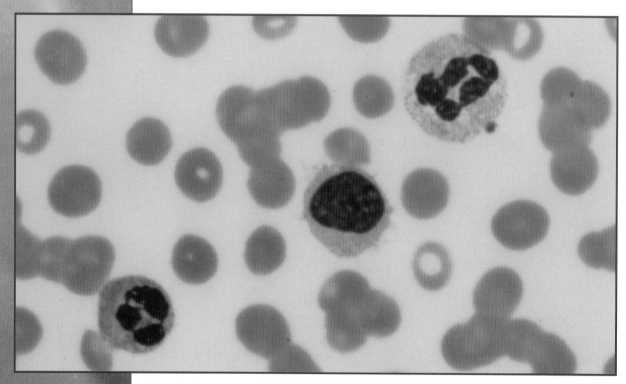

The dark cell in the center of this image is a leukocyte of hairy cell leukemia. The lighter-colored cells are red blood cells.

Diseases of the Blood

There are a number of diseases that specifically affect the blood. Among the most severe are anemia and leukemia. Anemia is a condition in which there is a decline in the blood's ability to carry oxygen. This is because the blood lacks the normal amount of red blood cells, hemoglobin, or both. Each red blood cell contains a large amount of hemoglobin, a protein that can bind with oxygen molecules.

In healthy people, the number of red blood cells remains constant because of a balance between red cell production and destruction. Anemia results if this balance is disturbed. The condition causes people to suffer weakness, breathlessness, and to look pale.

Leukemia, a form of cancer, is a much more life-threatening condition than anemia, and involves an abnormal increase in the number of white blood cells. The exact causes of leukemia are not yet known, but it is often fatal. The disease can result from viruses attacking the body or from prolonged exposure to radioactive materials or certain chemicals.

4
The Lymphatic and Immune Systems

Two other bodily systems are closely connected to the circulatory system. They are the lymphatic and immune systems. The lymphatic system guards the body against sickness and disease. Lymph is a pale fluid that is gathered from body tissues by a network of tiny vessels. It carries cells that fight germs and is cleaned in what are called lymph nodes. Lymph nodes are tiny, long, bean-shaped enlargements of lymph vessels. They are found in various parts the body such as the neck, armpits, and groin.

If germs enter the body, white cells in the lymph nodes multiply, and the lymph nodes swell up and can be felt as tender bulges under the skin. Their swelling is a sign that the body is fighting an infection. The white cells in lymph nodes are called memory lymphocytes. They are present at all times to attack germs that may enter the body. They may live in the lymph nodes for more than ten years. The body also has lymphlike tissues called lymphoid tissue. These tissues can be found in the adenoids at the back of the nasal cavity, and in the tonsils in the throat. They are also located in the appendix and large intestine. They work like lymph nodes, to filter and clean the blood.

Another organ that plays a part in the lymphatic system is the spleen. The largest organ in the lymphatic system, it is a dark purple, spongy, kidney-shaped organ about five inches (thirteen centimeters) long. It is located in the upper left part of the abdomen, behind the stomach, and at the lower ribs. The spleen contains many lymphocytes that "eat" germs. They do this by making antibodies and releasing them into the bloodstream to keep the body healthy. The spleen also breaks down worn-

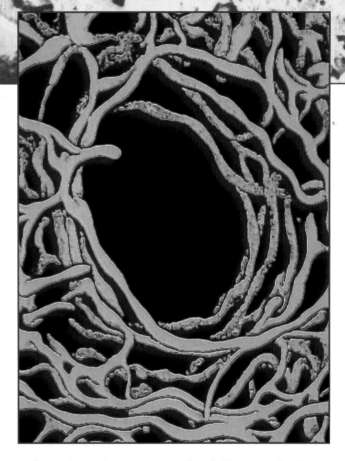

The spleen has a network of fibers, called the trabeculae, that allows for the proper functions of the spleen, such as regulating the number of red blood cells circulating in the bloodstream.

out red blood cells and platelets. It recycles their contents to the bone marrow, liver, and other organs. It also breaks down small blood clots.

AIDS and the Lymph System

Acquired immune deficiency syndrome, or AIDS, is a viral infection that has become a worldwide epidemic, causing the deaths of millions of people. One of the first signs of AIDS is its attack on the lymphatic system.

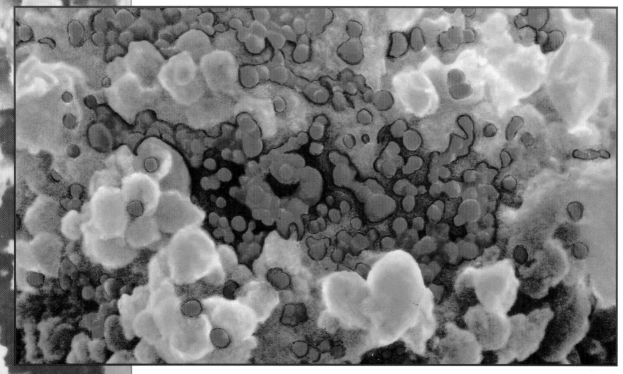

This white blood cell has been infected with HIV, shown in red. HIV, the causative agent of AIDS, attaches itself to cells and reproduces quickly, overwhelming the immune system.

The AIDS virus is called HIV, or human immuno-deficiency virus. If it enters the body, it can remain there for years with no harmful effects. When the virus multiplies, white cells in the body also multiply and try to fight the virus. This causes the lymph nodes to swell up. Gradually, however, the virus disables the white cells. That damages the body's immune system, which can no longer fight off other infections.

The Immune System

The immune system is also designed to fight disease and keep the body healthy. Germs that invade the body contain chemicals called antigens. The memory lymphocytes in the lymphatic and circulatory systems produce anti-bodies, chemicals designed to attach themselves to and kill specific germs. When a germ enters the body, the immune system can kill it before it can multiply and make the person ill.

Modern medicine has found ways to keep germs from making people unhealthy through vaccinations. A weakened or dead form of a virus is injected into the body, and the immune system manufactures antibodies to destroy it. These antibodies remain in the body and protect it from further infections for years.

Remember the last time you were vaccinated at your doctor's office or at school? You may have been vaccinated to make your body immune to measles, mumps, tetanus, polio, diphtheria, or whooping cough. Flu shots can be taken to prevent or lessen the severity of getting influenza. But a person can still catch the flu; the body may not recognize all the different types of flu virus even after immunization.

5

Disorders of the Circulatory System

Two of the most serious disorders of the circulatory system are arteriosclerosis and hypertension. Arteriosclerosis is a disease that results from the accumulation of fatty deposits in the arteries. The fat stiffens and thickens the arterial walls. This restricts the flow of blood through the arteries. Sometimes, blood clots develop in blood vessels that are partially blocked by fatty deposits, and this may cause a heart attack or stroke.

Hypertension is more commonly called high blood pressure. The condition is often associated with arteriosclerosis, since restrictions to blood flow will raise blood pressure. Hypertension makes the heart work harder. It may lead to a heart attack, a stroke, or kidney failure. A heart attack can occur when a blood clot gets wedged in a coronary artery and blocks the flow of blood to the heart muscle itself. The part of the heart muscle that receives blood from this artery becomes damaged from the lack of oxygen. This can cause the heart to stop beating. Doctors can see if this condition exists by taking an X ray image called an angiogram. This is done by injecting a dye into the bloodstream that shows up under X rays.

Blood Pressure

It is important for adults to have their blood pressure measured about once a year. Early detection of high blood pressure can save a person's life by preventing a heart attack or stroke. To measure blood pressure, a doctor or nurse ties a rubber bladder wrapped in cloth around a person's arm. They then pump this bag full of air until it cuts off the flow of blood

Arteriosclerosis, or the hardening of the arteries, keeps blood from flowing easily throughout the body. The thickening of arterial walls is often caused by a high-fat diet and smoking.

in the brachial artery, a large artery in the arm. The medic then listens to the artery inside the elbow. To hear better, he or she uses an amplifying instrument called a stethoscope.

When the air pressure closes the artery, there is no sound, because no blood can get through. The medic then gradually releases the pressure. When it is low enough so blood can pass, a tapping sound is heard in the stethoscope. This is called the systolic pressure. As the pressure continues to fall, the artery opens wide and the sound of blood flow becomes quieter, and then disappears. This is recorded as the diastolic pressure. It is written as a fraction,

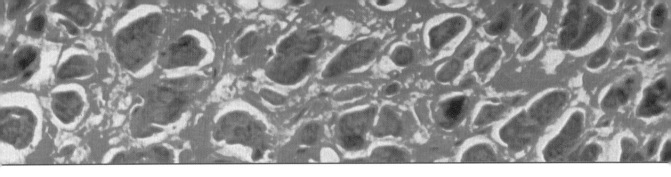

with the systolic pressure over the diastolic pressure. Normal blood pressure is about 100–120 millimeters of mercury over 70–80 mm.

Doctors treat arteriosclerosis and hypertension by recommending rest, moderate exercise, and changes in one's diet. Various drugs may also be prescribed to lower a person's blood pressure, to strengthen their heart, or to prevent infection and blood clots. In very serious cases, a surgeon may remove clots or replace one or more diseased blood vessels.

Other disorders of the circulatory system occur because of damage or defects in the heart or blood vessels. A bacterial infection may harm or destroy the valves that control the flow of blood through the heart. Damage or defects in the heart can be corrected by surgery.

Keeping the Heart Healthy

In order to keep your heart and circulatory system healthy, doctors recommend the following:

- Avoid being overweight or underweight. Too much weight puts a strain on the heart, making it work harder to pump blood around all the extra tissue in the body. Dieting that causes a sudden loss of weight is also bad for the heart.

- Eat a balanced diet with lots of fruits and vegetables.

- Don't eat a lot of foods that have a lot of fat, such as cheese and hamburgers. They taste good, but fat can block

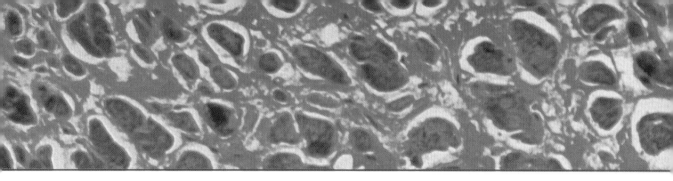

the arteries that supply blood to the heart's muscle. Instead of eating red meat every day, substitute tofu, chicken, turkey, or fish.

- Avoid eating too much sugar.
- Don't consume too much salt. It causes diseases like hypertension that can cause a heart attack.
- Get plenty of exercise every day. Exercise makes the bones stronger, and joints move and bend easier. Muscles also become bigger and stronger and are less likely to become stressed or injured. Exercise also makes your heart beat faster. Without exercise to stimulate your heart rate, your body would become unhealthy and waste away.
- Don't smoke. Smoking causes arteries to harden and deprives the lungs and other parts of the body of the oxygen and nutrients they need to function properly.
- Don't do drugs. Taking drugs can do more than just damage your circulatory system.
- Stress caused by worry, anger, or being anxious about things can be harmful to the heart. Get enough sleep, and don't let things upset or worry you too much.

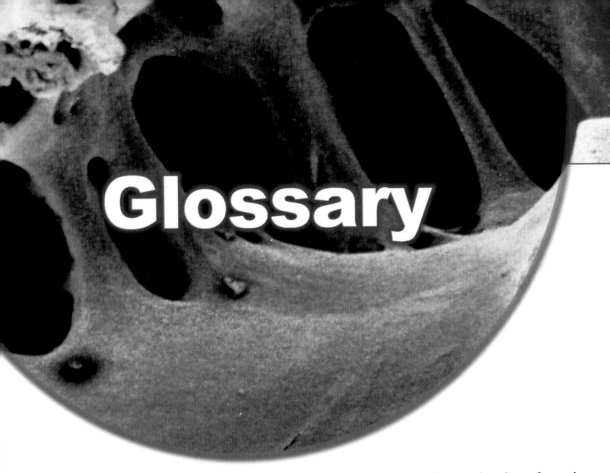

Glossary

anemia   A weakened condition caused by a lack of red blood cells, hemoglobin, or both.

antibodies   Proteins that attack germs in the body.

aorta   The large artery that carries blood away from the heart.

arteries   Blood vessels that carry blood away from the heart.

blood   A red liquid carried by blood vessels through the body.

blood vessels   Tiny tubes carrying blood between the heart and other parts of the body.

capillaries   Tiny blood vessels that link arteries and veins.

carbon dioxide   A waste product resulting from cells burning sugars for energy.

clot   A thick soft lump formed from blood proteins that blocks the flow of blood cells.

heart   The organ that pumps blood around the body.

hemoglobin   A red pigment in the blood cells that carries oxygen.

hemorrhage   Heavy bleeding.

hormones   Chemical messengers that control body functions.

immunity   Protection against disease germs.

lymph   A watery liquid flowing through the lymphatic system.

lymph nodes   Tissues that produce lymphocytes.

lymphocytes   White blood cells that defend the body against germs.

plasma   The liquid part of blood.

platelets   Blood cell fragments that help blood to clot.

red blood cells   Cells containing hemoglobin that carry oxygen through the bloodstream.

valves   Flaps of tissue that control the flow of blood in the heart or veins.

veins   Blood vessels carrying blood to the heart.

white blood cells   Colorless cells that aid the body's defense against disease.

For More Information

In the United States

Alice! Columbia University's Health Education Program
Lerner Hall
2920 Broadway, 7th Floor
MC 2608
New York, NY 10027
Web site: http://www.alice.columbia.edu

American College of Cardiology
Heart House
9111 Old Georgetown Road
Bethesda, MD 20814-1699
(800) 253-4636
(301) 897-5400
Web site: http://www.acc.org

American Heart Association
7272 Greenville Avenue
Dallas, TX 75231
(800) AHA-USA1 (242-8721)
Web site: http://www.americanheart.org

Franklin Institute Science Museum
The Heart: An Online Exploration
222 North 20th Street
Philadelphia, PA 19103
(215) 448-1200
Web site: http://sln.fi.edu/biosci

Med Help International
Suite 130, Box 188
6300 North Wickham Road
Melbourne, FL 32940
(321) 733-0069
Web site: http://www.medhelp.org

National Heart, Lung, and Blood Institute
P.O. Box 30105
Bethesda, MD 20824-0105
(301) 592-8573
Web site: http://www.nhlbi.nih.gov

In Canada

Health Canada
A.L. 0904A
Ottawa, ON K1A 0K9
(613) 957-2991
Web site: http://www.hc-sc.gc.ca

Heart and Stroke Foundation of Canada
222 Queen Street, Suite 1402
Ottawa, ON K1P 5V9
(613) 569-4361
Web site: http://www.heartandstroke.ca

Web Sites

BioMedNet
http://www.bmn.com

BrainPOP.com
http://www.brainpop.com

Canadian Medical Association
http://www.cma.ca

Canadian Women's Health Network
http://www.cwhn.ca/indexeng.html

Cardiac Care Network of Ontario
http://www.ccn.on.ca

CardioSource
http://www.cardiosource.com

Congenital Heart Disease Information
http://www.tchin.org

Heart and Circulatory System—Health for Kids
http://kidshealth.about.com

Heart of the Matter
http://www.heartofthematter.org

Mayo Clinic Health Center
http://www.mayohealth.org

National Heart Council
http://www.nemahealth.org/heartcouncil.html

StayHealthy.com
http://www.stayhealthy.com

University of Ottawa Heart Institute
http://www.ottawaheart.ca

For Further Reading

Avraham, Regina. *The Circulatory System.* New York: Chelsea House, 1999.

Ballard, Carol. *The Heart and Circulatory System.* Austin: Raintree/Steck-Vaughn, 1997.

Day, Trevor. *The Random House Book of 1001 Questions and Answers About the Human Body.* New York: Random House, 1994.

Gaskin, John. *The Heart.* New York: Franklin Watts, 1985.

LeMaster, Leslie Jean. *Your Heart and Blood.* Chicago: Children's Press, 1984.

Parker, Steve. *How the Body Works.* Pleasantville, NY: Reader's Digest Books, 1994.

Saunderson, Jane. *Heart and Lungs.* Mahwah, NJ: Troll Associates, 1992.

Silverstein, Alvin, Virginia Silverstein, and Robert Silverstein. *The Circulatory System.* New York: Twenty-First Century Books, 1994.

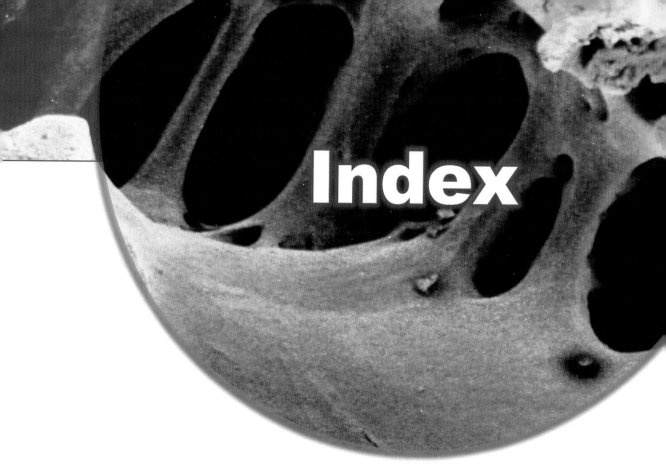

Index

F
food/nutrients, 4, 6, 9, 17, 18, 36–37

G
germs, 22, 30, 31, 32, 33

H
healthy, keeping, 36–37
heart, 4, 5, 6, 7, 8, 9, 10–17, 18, 26, 34, 36
 atria, 13
 chambers of, 13, 14, 15
 facts about, 12
 keeping it healthy, 36–37
 pumps of, 10–11
 transplants, 15
 valves of, 14–15, 36
 ventricles, 13
heart attack, 34, 35, 37
heartbeat, 12, 14, 17
heart bypass surgery, 16–17
hematologic system, 9
hemoglobin, 21, 27, 28
HIV, 32
hormones, 5, 18
hypertension/high blood pressure, 34, 35, 37

I
ill, becoming, 6, 33
immune system, 30, 32–33
infection, 5, 20, 22, 30, 31, 33, 36

K
kidneys, 10, 27
 failure of, 34

L
leukemia, 28–29
liver, 6, 31

lungs, 6, 7, 8, 9, 10–11, 13, 18, 21, 27, 37
lymphatic system, 30–31, 32–33
lymph nodes, 9, 30, 32
lymphocytes, 30, 31, 32–33

O
organs, 5, 9, 10, 18, 20, 22
oxygen, 4, 5, 8, 9, 10, 11, 17, 18, 21, 28, 34, 37

P
pacemaker, 16
plasma, 20–21, 26
platelets, 21, 22, 26, 31
proteins, 20, 21, 24, 28
pulmonary circulation, 6
pulse, taking your, 17

R
respiratory system, 9
Rh system, 24

S
shock, 26
spleen, 9, 22, 31
stroke, 34, 35
systemic circulation, 6

V
vaccination, 33
valve replacement, 15
veins, 5, 8, 9, 11, 14, 17, 18, 24, 26, 27
 coronary, 10
 pulmonary, 9, 11
viruses, 29, 31, 32, 33

W
waste products, 5, 7, 9, 18

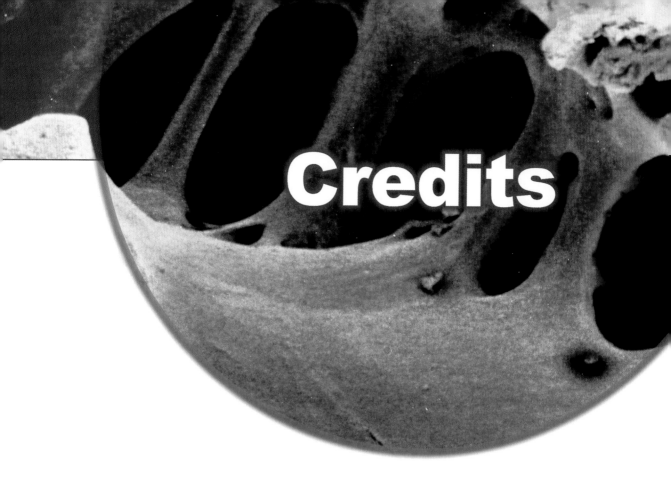

Credits

About the Author

Walter Oleksy has written over forty books for middle school readers and young adults on a wide range of subjects. His books for Rosen include *The Nervous System*, *Careers in Web Design*, and *Careers in Agriculture*. His other books include *Lincoln's Unknown Private Life*, *Hispanic-American Scientists*, and biographies of Christopher Reeve, Princess Diana, and James Dean. He is now writing four books on maps—maps in history, uses of maps at sea and in the skies, and map-making. Oleksy lives in a Chicago suburb with his dog Max, a mix of black Labrador retriever and German shepherd, who is now fourteen years old and still likes to run and sniff in the nearby woods.

Photo Credits

P. 5 © Life ART; p. 7 © Quest/Science Photo Library/Photo Researchers, Inc.; pp. 8, 11, 15, and 16 © Science Photo Library/Photo Researchers, Inc.; p. 13 © Life ART; p. 19 © Dr. Kari Lounatmaa/Science Photo Library/Photo Researchers, Inc.; pp. 20, 23 © Dr. Gopal Murti/Science Photo Library/Photo Researchers, Inc.; p. 27 © Scott Camazine/Photo Researchers, Inc.; p. 28 © SPL/Custom Medical Stock; p. 31 © Alfred Pasieka/Science Photo Library/Photo Researchers, Inc.; p. 32

Series Design

Cindy Williamson

Layout

Danielle Goldblatt